25 Remedies for the Sick

from the Risale-i Nur Collection
Humanity's Encounter with the Divine Series

25
Remedies
for the Sick

* Twenty-fifth Gleam

Bediüzzaman
SAİD NURSİ

TUGHRA
BOOKS
New Jersey

Published by Tughra Books
26 Worlds Fair Dr. Unit C
Somerset, New Jersey, 08873, USA

www.tughrabooks.com

Translated from Turkish by Hüseyin Akarsu

ISBN: 978-1-59784-218-1

Printed by
Ayhan Matbaa Istanbul - Turkey

Table of Contents

Bediüzzaman and the Risale-i Nur

In the many dimensions of his lifetime of achievement, as well as in his personality and character, Bediüzzaman (1877-1960) was and, through his continuing influence, still is an important thinker and writer in the Muslim world. He represented in a most effective and profound way the intellectual, moral and spiritual strengths of Islam, evident in different degrees throughout its fourteen-century history. He lived for eighty-five years. He spent almost all of those years, overflowing with love and ardor for the cause of Islam, in a wise and measured activism based on sound reasoning and in the shade of the Qur'an and the Prophetic example.

Bediüzzaman lived in an age when materialism was at its peak and many crazed after communism, and the world was in great crisis. In that critical period, Bediüzzaman pointed people to the source of belief and inculcated in them a strong hope for a collective restoration. At a time when science and philosophy were used to mislead young generations into atheism, and nihilistic attitudes had a wide appeal, at a time when all this was done in the name of civilization, modernization and contemporary thinking and those who tried to resist them were subjected to the cruelest of persecutions, Bediüzzaman strove for the overall revival of a whole people, breathing into their minds and spirits whatever is taught in the institutions of both modern and traditional education and of spiritual training.

Bediüzzaman had seen that modern unbelief originated from science and philosophy, not from ignorance as previously. He wrote that nature is the collection of Divine signs and therefore science and religion cannot be conflicting disciplines. Rather, they are two (apparently) different expressions of the same truth. Minds should be enlightened with sciences, while hearts need to be illumined by religion.

Bediüzzaman was not a writer in the usual sense of the word. He wrote his splendid work the *Risale-i Nur*, a collection exceeding 5,000 pages, because he had a mission: he struggled against the materialistic and atheistic trends of thought fed by science and philosophy and tried to present the truths of Islam to modern minds and hearts of every level of understanding. The *Risale-i Nur*, a modern commentary of the Qur'an, mainly concentrates on the existence and unity of God, the Resurrection, Prophethood, the Divine Scriptures primarily including the Qur'an, the invisible realms of existence, Divine Destiny and humanity's free will, worship, justice in human life, and humanity's place and duty among the creation.

In order to remove from pople's minds and hearts the accumulated 'sediment' of false beliefs and conceptions and to purify them both intellectually and spiritually, Bediüzzaman writes forcefully and makes reiterations. He writes in neither an academic nor a didactic way; rather he appeals to feelings and aims to pour out his thoughts and ideas into people's hearts and minds in order to awaken them to belief and conviction.

This book includes selected sections from the *Risale-i Nur* collection.

Twenty-five remedies for those who are ill

[from *The Gleams*, the Twenty-fifth Gleam]

This treatise was written as a medicine, a solace, a spiritual prescription, and as a visit wishing recovery for those who are ill.

A reminder and an apology

This spiritual prescription, which was written at great speed, has not been revised and has been left as it occurred to my heart. Therefore, I request the readers, and particularly the unwell, not to feel offended by any disagreeable expressions that may be contained within. I also request them to pray for me.

> Those who, when a disaster befalls them, say, "Surely we belong to God (as His creatures and servants), and surely to Him we are bound to return." (2: 156)

> "And He it is Who gives me food and drink; And Who, when I fall ill, heals me." (26: 79–80)

In this Gleam, we explain the twenty-five remedies which may offer true consolation for those who are ill or struck by misfortune, who make up one tenth of humankind.

The first remedy

You who are unhappy in your sickness! Do not be anxious, persevere instead. Your illness is not a loss for you, but a gain, a sort of cure. For life departs like capital. If it yields no fruits, it is wasted. And if it passes in ease and heedlessness, it is short, bringing almost no profit. Illness makes that capital of yours yield huge profits. Moreover, it prevents your life from being short; it holds it back, lengthening or expanding it, so that it may depart after yielding its fruits. Indicating the fact that life lengthens through illness, this proverb is much renowned and widely circulated: "The time of disaster is very long; the time of enjoyment, very short."

The second remedy

You who are ill and lacking in perseverance! Do indeed persevere and offer thanks. Your illness may transform each of the minutes of your life that pass in illness into one hour's worship. For worship is of two sorts. One is that which is performed, the other is the sort which is not actually performed, but is suffered and thus leads to sincere supplication. Illnesses and disasters are examples of this sort. By means of these, those afflicted deeply feel their innate impotence and weakness; they take refuge in their All-Compassionate Creator and entreat, thus being able to perform sincere worship. There are authenticated narrations from God's noble Messenger, upon him be peace and blessings, that the times of believers which pass in illness are counted as worship, provided they do not complain about God.[1] It is also reliably narrated from the Messenger and there are reports from saints of spiritual discovery that one minute's illness of some patients who show perseverance with thankfulness equals one hour's worship, and a minute's illness of certain spiritually perfected individuals, equals the worship of a day. Therefore, rather than complaining, be thankful for the illness, which makes one minute of your life the equivalent of a thousand minutes and gains for you a long life.

The third remedy

You who are impatient in your illness! The fact that all those who come to this world inevitably depart, that the young grow old, and that the world is perpetually turning amidst death and separation, testifies that humankind has not come to this world for enjoyment or pleasure. In addition, although humankind is the most perfect of living beings, the richest of beings in the equipment of life, and can virtually be regarded as their king, because of dwelling on past pleasures and worrying about future troubles, human beings lead a grievous, troublesome life, much lower than the animals. This shows that humankind has not come to this world to live in ease and pleasure. Rather, possessing vast capital, it has come here to work for an eternal life

---

[1] al-Bukhari, "Jihad" 134; Ahmad ibn Hanbal, *al-Musnad*, 4:410. (Tr.)

by doing the required trade. The capital given to it is its lifetime.

Were it not for illness, good health and ease would cause heedlessness, presenting the world as pleasant and making people oblivious of the Hereafter. By distracting them from the thought of death and the grave, good health and ease cause them to waste the capital of life on trifles. But illness suddenly gives them awareness, and says to the body: "You are not immortal, and have not been left to your own devices. You have a duty. Give up haughtiness; think of the One Who has created you; know that you will enter the grave, and make the necessary preparation!" Thus, from this perspective, illness is an advisor that never deceives; and it is an admonishing guide. For this reason, rather than complaining about illness, we should be thankful for it. If it gives much trouble and pain, we should show patience.

The fourth remedy

You who are ill and complaining! It is better for you not to complain, but to give thanks and show patience. For your body, with all its members and your faculties, is not your property. You have not made them, nor have you bought any of your bodily components from any workshop. They are the property of someone else. Their Owner has disposal over His property as He wills.

As stated in The Twenty-Sixth Word (included in *The Words*), a very rich and infinitely skilled clothes designer uses an ordinary man as a model to display his works of art and invaluable wealth in return for wages. For a brief hour, he clothes the model in a jeweled and artistically fashioned garment that he has made. He continues to modify the garment while the model wears it. In order to display his wonderful varieties of art, he cuts the garment, alters it, lengthening it here and shortening it there. Does the model employed for a wage have any right to say, "Your orders to bow and stand up are causing me trouble. Your cutting and shortening of this garment, which must make me more beautiful, spoils my beauty"? Can the model accuse the designer of treating him unkindly and unfairly?

You who are ill! As in that simile, the All-Majestic Maker—in order to display the embroideries of His All-Beautiful Names and indeed make you more and more "beautiful"—causes you to undergo numerous, different states and situations in the garment of your body in which He has clothed you, bejeweled as it is with luminous faculties like seeing, hearing, reasoning, and feeling. Just as, through hunger, you learn of His Name, The All-Providing, so too through your illness, you come to know His Name, The All-Healing. Since suffering and disasters manifest the decrees and operations of some of His Names, there are in them gleams of wisdom, and rays of mercy, within which are numerous beauties. If the veil between us and His decrees and acts were to be lifted, you would find many agreeable and beautiful meanings behind the veil of illness, which you are frightened of and dislike.

The fifth remedy

You who are afflicted with illness! I have become convinced through experience at this time that illness is a Divine favor for some people, a gift of mercy. Although I am not worthy of it, for these last eight or nine years, a number of young people have visited me to pray for them because of their illnesses. I have noticed that compared to those of the same age, any unwell young person I have met has begun to think of the Hereafter. They are no longer in the typical intoxication of youth, and have saved themselves to a degree from the animal desires that are embedded in heedlessness. Based on this observation, I would remind them that their bearable illnesses are a Divine favor. I would say, "Brother, I am not opposed to this illness of yours. I do not feel compassion for you due to your illness, so that I should pray for you. Try to show good patience until illness awakens you completely, and after it has completed its duty, God willing, the All-Compassionate Creator will cure you."

I would also say to them as follows:

> Because of the calamity of good health, some of your
> equals in age become heedless, and do not perform
> the five daily Prayers; they do not think of the grave,
> forget God, and damage, even destroy, the eternal life
> for the sake of the superficial pleasure of an hour's
> worldly life. But with the eye of illness, you see your
> grave, which you will in any case enter, and the man-
> sions of the Hereafter beyond it, and act accordingly.
> This means that illness is good health for you, while
> the good health of some of your peers is in fact an ill-
> ness for them.

The sixth remedy

You who are sick and complain of your suffering, I
say to you: Think of your past life and remember the
pleasurable, happy days and the distressing, troubled
times. For sure, you will either say, "Oh!" or, "Ah!"
That is, your heart and tongue will either say, "All
praise and thanks be to God!" or, "Alas, alas!"

Notice that what makes you utter a sigh of relief
and say, "All praise and thanks be to God!" is that your
thinking of the sufferings and calamities that befell
you in the past stirs up a kind of spiritual pleasure and
causes your heart to be thankful. For the disappearance of suffering is a pleasure. The passing of sufferings and calamities left a lasting pleasure in the spirit.
When it is stirred up through thinking, a pleasure pours
forth from the spirit with thanks.

What makes you exclaim, "Alas, alas!" is the pleasurable and happy times you enjoyed in the past. Through cessation, they have left an unending pain in your spirit so that whenever you think of them, that pain is aroused and causes sorrow and regret to pour forth.

Since one day's illicit pleasure sometimes causes a year's spiritual suffering, while the pain of one day's temporary illness brings the pleasure of many days' rewards together with the pleasure of its cessation, think of the result of this temporary illness you are suffering now and the rewards it potentially bears. Say, "This too will pass, God willing!" and, instead of complaining, offer thanks.

Another sixth remedy

You, brother or sister in faith, who think of the pleasures of this world and are distressed by illness! If this world were eternal, and if on our way to eternity there were no death, and if the winds of separation and death did not blow, and if there were no "winters" of the spirit in the calamitous and stormy future, I would have pitied you along with you. But since the world will one day say to us, "Now, it is the time of departure!" and close its ears to our cries, warned by these illness, we must give up our love of it before it drives us out. Before it abandons us, we must try to abandon it in our hearts.

Illness reminds us of this reality and says, "Your body is not composed of stone and iron; rather it has been composed of various materials that are subject to partition and dissolution. Give up conceit, be aware of your innate impotence, recognize your Master, know your duties, and learn why you came to the world!" Illness says this secretly in the ear of the heart.

Also, since the pleasure and enjoyment of this world do not last and, particularly if they are licit, this is distressing and painful, do not weep over their disappearance because of illness. On the contrary, think of the worship you are performing by enduring the illness and the rewards that pertain to the Hereafter, and try to be content.

The seventh remedy

You who are ill and have lost the pleasures of health! Your illness does not ruin the contentment of the Divine blessing in health; rather, it causes you to taste it more deeply, and increases it. For if something continues uninterruptedly, it loses its effect. The people of truth agree that "things are known through their opposites." For example, were it not for darkness, light would not be known and it would give no pleasure. Without cold, heat would not be recognized, and would remain unpleasant. If there were no hunger, food would offer no delight. If there were no thirst, drinking water would give no satisfaction. Without illness, health and appetite would be without pleasure.

By endowing humans with numerous senses, organs, and faculties that they may taste and recognize the uncountable varieties of His bounties in the universe, the All-Wise Originator shows that He wills that humans may experience all the varieties of His bounties and give continual thanks. Therefore, as He grants good health and appetite, He will certainly give illnesses and pains. I ask you: If you were not suffering this discomfort in your head or hands or stomach, would you be mindful of the pleasure of the Divine favor of the good health in your head or hands or stomach, and offer thanks? Certainly, not only would you not have offered thanks, you would not have even considered it! You would have expended that good health unconsciously and heedlessly, and perhaps even wantonly.

The eighth remedy

You who are sick and now reflecting on the Hereafter! Like soap, sickness washes away the dirt of sins and cleanses. It is established in an authenticated hadith that illnesses are expiation for sins. It says, "As ripe fruits fall from the tree when it is shaken, so the sins of a believer fall away with the shaking during illness."[2]

---

[2] al-Bukhari, "Marda'" 1, 2, 13; Muslim, "Birr" 14. (Tr.)

Sins are perpetual illnesses in the eternal life. They are also illnesses for the heart, conscience, and spirit in this worldly life. If you persevere and do not complain, you are being saved from numerous perpetual illnesses through that temporary illness. But if you do not worry about sins, or are not aware of the afterlife, or do not recognize God, you have such an illness that it is a million times worse than your present illness. Cry out at it, for your heart, spirit, and soul have relations with all the beings in the world. Your connections with them are continually severed through decay, death, and separation, causing innumerable wounds to open up in you. Particularly since you are not aware of the Hereafter and imagine death to be eternal extinction, it is as if you had a body afflicted with uncountable wounds and illnesses. Therefore, what you must do first is to search for belief as the cure for these innumerable spiritual wounds and illnesses of the ailing body. You must correct your creed, and the shortest, most direct way to such a cure is to recognize the Power and Mercy of an All-Powerful One of Majesty through the window of your innate impotence and weakness, which your physical illness shows you beneath the veil of heedlessness that it has rent.

Indeed, one who does not recognize God is afflicted with a worldful of tribulations, while the world of one who recognizes God is full of light and spiritual joy.

Everyone is aware of this according to the strength of their belief. The pain of physical illnesses melts away under the spiritual joy, healing, and pleasure that come from belief.

The ninth remedy

You who are ill and who acknowledge your Creator! People fear and are distressed by illness because it sometimes leads to death. Since death is frightening to the superficial, heedless view, illnesses that may lead to it cause fear and worry.

So, first of all, know and believe with certainty that the appointed hour of death is certain and does not change. It has many times occurred that the healthy ones weeping beside the seriously ill have died, while the seriously ill have been cured and continue to live.

Secondly, death is not frightening; it is not as it appears to be. Based on the light provided by the wise Qur'an, we have convincingly explained in many parts of the *Risale-i Nur* that for people of belief, death is a discharge from the hardship of the duties of this life. It is also a respite from worship, which is a drill and training in the arena of trials in this world. Moreover, it is a means of reunion with ninety-nine relatives and beloved ones who have already emigrated to the other world. It is also a means of entering the true homeland and eternal abode of happiness. In addition, it is an invitation from the prison of the world to the spacious gardens of Paradise. And it is the time when one receives a wage from the grace of the All-Compassionate Creator in return for a service. Since this is the reality of death, we should view death not as something terrifying, but as the prelude to mercy and happiness.

Moreover, for some of the people of God, the fear of death is not terror of death itself, but rather on account of their hope, through the continuation of the duties of life, that they will gain more merit by performing more good works.

For the people of belief, death is the door to Divine mercy, while for the people of misguidance it is the pit of eternal darkness.

The tenth remedy

You who are ill and worrying needlessly! Your worry is because of the severity of your illness, but your worries make your illness more severe. If you want your illness to be less severe, try not to worry about it. That is, think about the benefits of your illness, the spiritual rewards it brings, and that it will pass quickly. Give up worrying, and cut off the illness at the root.

Indeed, worry doubles the burden of illness; in addition to your physical illness, it causes an immaterial illness in your heart, upon which the physical illness

depends and through which it persists. If that worry
vanishes through submission, resignation, and thinking
of the wisdom inherent in the illness, one of the important roots of the illness will be severed. It becomes
less severe and in part disappears. Sometimes a minor
physical illness becomes tenfold just through worries
and apprehension. When worries and apprehension
cease, nine tenths of the illness disappears. In addition
to increasing an illness, since worry is an accusation
against Divine wisdom, a criticism of Divine Mercy,
and a complaint about the All-Compassionate Creator,
it causes counter-suffering, and increases illness.

Indeed, just as thankfulness increases favor, so too
do complaints increase illnesses and suffering. Furthermore, worry is itself an illness. The cure for it is
knowing the wisdom inherent in illness. Since you are
now aware of the wisdom in illness and its benefits,
apply that ointment to the worry and be relieved. Say,
"Oh!" instead of, "Ah!" and "All praise be to God for
every state!" instead of, "Alas!" and "Oh dear!"

The eleventh remedy

You, brother or sister in faith! You who are sick and
impatient! Although your present illness causes you
some suffering, all your former illnesses have produced
an immaterial contentment for your spirit resulting in
your recovery from them, and a spiritual pleasure aris-

ing from the reward received for enduring them. There
may be no more illnesses from today on, even from
this hour, so no pain can come from something that
does not exist. And if there is no pain, there is no grief.
But since you imagine otherwise, you are showing impatience. For all the times of illness before today have
disappeared together with the pains they have caused,
leaving the rewards the illness has brought and the
pleasure their departure gives. So, when they should
give you the feeling of profit and happiness, it is crazy
to think of them and feel grieved, or to be impatient.
The future days have not come yet. Thinking of them
now and feeling grieved and showing impatience with
thoughts about a day that does not exist, or an illness
that does not exist, or a suffering that does not exist,
and thus giving the color of existence to three degrees
of non-existence—if that is not crazy, what is?

Since the times of illness before now have given
happiness, and since the times subsequent to it and the
illnesses and sufferings (you imagine they may bring)
are non-existent, do not scatter the power of the patience God Almighty has given you to the right and
left, but mobilize it against the pain of the present
hour. Say, "O All-Patient One!" and endure it.

The twelfth remedy

You who on account of illness cannot perform your
regular worship or invocations, and regret this! Know

that it is stated in a *hadith*, "A pious, God-revering believer who, due to illness, cannot do the invocations he does normally and regularly, receives an equal reward."[3] Illness substitutes for the supererogatory Prayers of the ill person who does their obligatory worship as much as possible and shows patience in submissive reliance on God.

Furthermore, illness reminds people of their innate impotence and weakness, and causes them to pray both verbally and through the tongue of their state. God Almighty has created human beings with boundless impotence and weakness so that they continually seek refuge in the Divine Court and pray and supplicate. Since, according to the verse, *Say: "My Lord would not care for you were it not for your prayer,"* (25:77) the wisdom in the creation of humanity and the reason for its value are sincere prayer, and as illness leads people to such prayers, rather than complaining about illness, we should thank God, and should not turn off the fountain of prayer that has been caused to flow by illnesses.

The thirteenth remedy

You who are unhappy and complain of your illness! Illness is an important treasure and a very valuable Divine gift for some people. Every ill person can consider their illness from this perspective.

---

[3] Abu Dawud, "Jana'iz" 1; Ahmad ibn Hanbal, *al-Musnad*, 4:418.(Tr.)

Our appointed hour of death is unknown to us. So, in order to save people from absolute despair and heedlessness and to keep them between fear and hope and in a position from which they may lose neither in the world nor in the Hereafter, God Almighty has concealed the appointed hour of death. Since death can come at any time, if it captures the human being in heedlessness, it may cause great harm to their eternal life. But illness dispels heedlessness, makes people think of their afterlife and reminds them of death and thus prepares them for the Hereafter. They sometimes make such great profit that in twenty days they can gain a rank that they could not otherwise have gained in twenty years.

For instance, from among my friends there were two youths, may God have mercy on them, Sabri from the village of Ilema, and Vezirzade Mustafa from Islamköy. I used to note with amazement that although these two were illiterate and could not serve by copying the *Risale-i Nur*, they were among the foremost in sincerity and the service of belief. I did not know why that was so. After their deaths I understood that both had suffered from a serious illness. Guided by that illness, unlike other heedless youths who did not carry out the obligatory worship, they had great reverence for God, and performed the most valuable services, attaining a state beneficial to the Hereafter. God willing, the trouble of two years' illness was the means to the bliss of millions of years of eternal life. I now understand that the prayers I sometimes offered for their health were maledictions in respect to this world. I hope that my prayers were accepted for their well-being in the Hereafter.

Thus, it is my belief that these two gained a profit equal to that which can be gained through ten years' piety and righteousness (*taqwa*). If, like some young people, they had trusted in their youth and good health and let themselves fall into heedlessness and dissipation, and if death, which is always on the watch, had grasped them right in the midst of the filth of their sins, their graves would have been the lairs of scorpions and snakes, instead of that treasury of lights.

Since there are such benefits in illness, we should not complain about it, but bear it with patient reliance on God, indeed, with gratitude to Him and confidence in His Mercy.

The fourteenth remedy

You who are sick in that your eyes are afflicted with cataracts! If you knew what a light and spiritual seeing there is beneath the cataracts that may cover a believer's eyes, you would exclaim, "A hundred thousand thanks to my All-Compassionate Lord." I will relate an incident to you to explain this ointment. It is as follows:

One time, the aunt of Süleyman from Barla, who served me for eight years with perfect loyalty and without causing any resentment, became blind. Thinking well of me a hundred times more than was my due, that righteous woman caught me by the door of the mosque and asked me to pray for the recovery of her eyes. I therefore made that blessed woman's righteousness the intercessor for my prayer, and entreated, "O Lord! Restore her sight due to her righteousness." Two days later, an eye specialist from Burdur came and removed the cataracts. But forty days later she again lost her sight. I was much grieved and prayed for her earnestly. I hope that the prayer was accepted for her afterlife, or else my prayer was the most mistaken malediction for her. For there remained only another forty days until her death; forty days later she died— May God have mercy on her.

Thus, rather than looking sorrowfully at the pathetic gardens of Barla with the eye of old age, she profited by being able to gaze on the gardens of Paradise from her grave for forty thousand days, for she had a firm belief and was earnestly righteous.

If a believer loses their sight and enters the grave blind, they may, in accordance with their degree, gaze on the world of light to a much greater extent than the other people of the grave. Just as in this world we see many things that blind believers do not see, if they go from this world with belief, they see to a greater extent than the other people of the grave. As if looking through the most powerful telescopes, they can, in accordance with their degree, see and gaze on the gardens of Paradise as on a movie screen.

Thus, through thanks and patience you can find under the veil that exists on your present eye an eye that is light-filled and light-diffusing and with which you can see and gaze on Paradise above the heavens while under the soil. The eye specialist which will remove the veil from your present eye and enable you to look with that eye is the wise Qur'an.

The fifteenth remedy

You who are sick and sighing and lamenting! Do not consider the outward aspect of illness and sigh; consider its meaning and be content. If the meaning of illness was not good, the All-Compassionate Creator would not have given illness to His most-beloved servants. A *hadith* says, "Those afflicted with the severest trials are the Prophets, then those resembling them, and then those resembling the latter."[4] That is, those most afflicted with suffering and hardship are the best of people, the most perfect of them. The Prophets, including in particular the Prophet Job, upon him be peace, then the saints, and then those foremost in righ-

---

[4] at-Tirmidhi, "Zuhd" 57; Ibn Maja, "Fitan" 23. (Tr.)

teousness after the Prophets and saints have regarded the illnesses they have suffered as sincere worship and gifts from the All-Merciful. They have offered thanks in patience. They have seen these illnesses as surgical operations performed by the compassion of the All-Compassionate Creator.

O you who cry out and lament! If you want to join this light-diffusing caravan, offer thanks in patience. For if you complain, they will not admit you among them. You will fall into the pits of the people of misguidance, and go along a dark road.

Indeed, there are some illnesses which, if they lead to death, are like a sort of martyrdom. They cause one to gain some certain degree of sainthood. For example, like the believing women who die during or because of childbirth,[5] those who die from pains in the abdomen, and by drowning, burning, or the plague, are considered as martyrs.[6] There are also other such blessed illnesses which help to gain a degree of sainthood for those who die from them. Furthermore, since illness lessens the love of the world and attachment to it, it lightens the pain of parting from the world, which is extremely grievous for worldly people. Sometimes it makes such a departure desirable.

---

[5] A child-bearing woman may gain some sort of martyrdom if she dies within forty days after giving birth.

[6] al-Buhari, "Jihad" 30; Muslim, "'Imara" 164. (Tr.)

The sixteenth remedy

You who are sick and complain of your distress! Illness induces respect and compassion, which are most important and good for human social life. This saves people from conceited feelings of self-sufficiency, which drives them to unfriendliness and unkindness. For according to the reality stated in, *No indeed, but the human is unruly and rebels, in that he sees himself as self-sufficient* (96: 6–7), a carnal, evil-commanding soul which feels self-sufficient due to good health and well-being does not regard the many causes which are deserving of brotherhood. And they do not feel compassion towards the misfortune-stricken or ill, who should be shown kindness and pity. Yet, whenever they become ill, they are aware of their own innate impotence and neediness, and feel respect towards their sisters and brothers who are worthy of it. They pay respect to their believing brothers and sisters who visit or help them. And they feel human kindness, which originates in fellow-feeling and compassion for the disaster-stricken—a most important Islamic characteristic. Comparing others to themselves, they empathize with them, feel affection for them, and do whatever they can to help them. At the very least they pray for others and pay them a visit of consolation, which is a Sunna act according to the Shari'a,[7] thus earning reward.

---

[7] Muslim, "Birr" 40; Abu Dawud, "Jana'iz" 7; at-Tirmidhi, "Jana'iz" 2. (Tr.)

The seventeenth remedy

You who are sick and complain of not being able to do good works due to illness! Offer thanks! It is illness that opens to you the door of the most sincere of good works. Illness is a most important means of continuously gaining reward for the sick person and for those who are looking after them for the sake of God; it is, in addition, a means for supplications to be accepted.

Certainly, there is significant reward for believers who look after the sick. Asking after the health of those who are ill and visiting them—provided it does not tax them—is a sunna act, an act highly recommended by our Prophet, upon him be peace and blessings.[8] It is also expiation for sins. There is a hadith which says, "Receive the prayers of the ill, for their prayers are acceptable."[9]

Especially if the person who is ill is a relative, in particular parents, looking after them is an important form of worship which yields significant rewards. To please an invalid's heart and to console them is like giving alms. Fortunate is the one who pleases the easily-touched hearts of their father and mother when they are ill, and receives their prayer. Indeed, even the angels applaud saying, "How good, how blessed that

---

[8] al-Bukhari, "Marda'" 4, 5; Muslim, "Salam" 47. (Tr.)

[9] Ibn Maja "Jana'iz" 1; al-Bayhaqi, *Shu'ab al-Iman*, 6:541. (Tr.)

is! May God reward them abundantly!" before faithful scenes of those good offspring who respond to the compassion and care of their parents—those most worthy of respect in the life of society—during their illness with perfect respect and filial kindness, showing the exaltedness of humanity.

There is great happiness and joy during an illness which arises from the kindness, pity, and compassion of those around the one who is sick; they reduce the pains of the illness to nothing. The acceptability of the prayers of the sick is of great importance. For the past thirty or forty years, I myself have prayed to be cured of the lumbago from which I suffer. However, I understood that the illness was given to me as an encouragement to prayer. Since prayer cannot be removed through prayer, that is, since prayer cannot remove itself,[10] I understood that the answer to prayers will be obtained in the Hereafter, and that illness is itself a kind of worship, for through illness one realizes one's innate impotence and seeks refuge in the Divine Court. Therefore, although I have prayed for thirty years to be healed and apparently my prayer has not been accepted, it has never occurred to me to abandon the prayer. Because illness is the occasion or reason for prayer; to

---

[10] Certain illnesses encourage and are the reason for prayer. Therefore, if a prayer causes the termination of the illness, then prayer would annul the reason for it. This cannot be admitted.

be cured is not the effect of the prayer. If the All-Wise and Compassionate One bestows healing, He bestows it out of His pure grace.

Furthermore, if prayers are not accepted in the form we desire, it should not be said that they have not been answered. The All-Wise Creator knows better than us; He gives whatever is good for us. Sometimes in our interest He accepts our prayers for our worldly life in the name of our afterlife. In any event, a prayer that acquires sincerity due to an illness and which arises from our innate weakness, impotence, humility and need in particular, is very close to being acceptable. Illness is the means to the prayer that is sincere in this way. Both the sick who are religious and believers who look after the sick should make the most of this prayer.

The eighteenth remedy

You who are ill and have abandoned offering thanks and have now taken up complaining! Complaints arise from a right to complain. You have no rights violated, nor have you lost anything which would allow you to complain. Rather, there are numerous thanks that are obligatory for you, but you have not fulfilled them. Without performing your duties towards God Almighty, which are His rights over you, you are complaining as if you are demanding rights in a manner that is not righteous. You cannot look at others who are better off than you in health and complain. You are rather charged with looking at those who are worse than you in health, and offering thanks. If your hand is broken, look at those whose hands have been severed. If you have only one eye, look at those blind, lacking both eyes. And offer thanks to God!

Certainly, no one has the right to consider others as more advantaged than themselves in regard to bounties and to complain. And in tribulations, it is the right of all to consider those who are worse off than themselves, and thus offer thanks. This truth has been explained in a number of places in the *Risale-i Nur* with a simile, a summary of which is as follows:

A person conducts a poor wretch to the top of a minaret. At every step he gives the wretch a different gift, a different bounty. Right at the top of the minaret he gives him the largest gift. Although he deserves thanks and gratitude in return for all those various gifts, the churlish wretch forgets the gifts he has received at each step, or considers them of no importance, and without offering thanks, looks above him and begins to complain, saying: "If only this minaret had been higher, I could have climbed even further. Why isn't it as tall as that mountain over there or that other minaret?" If he begins to complain like this, what great ingratitude this is, what a great wrong!

In the same way, every human being comes into existence from nothing, and without being a rock or a tree or an animal, becomes human. Furthermore, being a Muslim is another great bounty. Most of the time, we enjoy good health and are honored with a great number of bounties. Despite all this, to complain and show impatience because we are not worthy of some bounties due to certain deficiencies pertaining to ourselves, or because we lose them through wrong choices or abuses, or because we were unable to obtain them, and thus to criticize the Divine Lordship, saying, "What have I done to cause this to happen to me?" is a spiritual sickness more disastrous than the physical one. Like fighting with a broken hand, complaint makes illness worse. The sensible person is the one who is proclaimed as,

> *Those who, when a disaster befalls them, say, "Surely we belong to God (as His creatures and servants), and surely to Him we are bound to return." (And they act accordingly)* (2: 156),

and shows patience in submission to God Almighty, so that the illness may complete its duty and depart.

The nineteenth remedy

As a term signifying God's being the Eternally Be-sought-of-All, while He Himself is in need of nothing, "the All-Beautiful Names" show that all the Names of the All-Gracious One of Majesty are beautiful. Among created beings, the most subtle, the most beautiful, the most comprehensive mirror that reflects God's being the Eternally Besought-of-All is life. The mirror to the beautiful is beautiful. The mirror that shows the beauties of the beautiful becomes beautiful. Just as whatever befalls the mirror through such beauty is good and beautiful, so also whatever befalls life, from the viewpoint of truth, is good, because it exhibits the beautiful imprints of the All-Beautiful Names, which are all good and beautiful.

If life passes monotonously with permanent health and appetite, it becomes a deficient mirror. Indeed, in one respect, it suggests non-existence and noth-ingness, and causes weariness. It reduces the value of life, and changes the pleasure of life into distress. With the intention of passing their time quickly, out of boredom people let themselves fall into either dis-sipation or into distractions. They become hostile to their valuable life as if it were a prison sentence, and want to kill it, and make it pass quickly. By contrast, a life that revolves in change and action and different states makes its value felt, and enables us to recog-nize its importance and pleasure. Even if it is a life of troubles and misfortune, one with such a life does not want life to pass quickly. They make no complaints out of boredom; they do not utter, "Alas! The sun hasn't set yet," or, "It is still night time."

Ask a rich and idle gentleman who is living in the lap of luxury with nothing lacking, "How are you?"

You will certainly hear a pathetic reply like, "Time never passes. Let's have a game of backgammon. Or let's find some other distraction to make time pass." Or else you will hear complaints arising from long-term worldly ambitions, like, "I haven't attained this; if only I had done that activity."

Then ask someone struck by disaster or a laborer or a poor man who is in hardship, "How are you?" If they are sensible, they will reply, "All thanks be to my Lord, I am well and working. If only the evening did not come so quickly, I could have finished this task! Time passes so quickly, and life goes on without stopping. Certainly, I have troubles and difficulties, but they will pass too. Everything passes quickly." In effect, such a person is saying how valuable life is and how they regret its passing. This means that they understand the pleasure and value of life which comes with hardship and labor, while ease and health make life bitter and make one desire for it to pass.

You, brother or sister Muslim, who are sick! As is explained convincingly and in detail in some other parts of the *Risale-i Nur*, know that the origin and culture of calamities and evils, and even of sins, is non-existence. As for non-existence, it is evil and darkness. It is because states like continuous ease, silence, inertia, and being sedentary are close to non-existence and nothingness that they make felt the darkness of non-existence and cause distress. As for action and change, they are existence and make existence felt. And existence is pure good, and it is light.

Since this is a reality, your illness has been sent to your body as a guest so that it will carry out many duties like purifying your valuable life, and strengthening and developing it, as well as making other members and faculties of your body turn in assistance towards the part of you that is unwell, and displaying the imprints of various Names of the All-Wise Maker. God willing, the illness will carry out its duties quickly and depart. And it will say to good health, "Now you come, and stay permanently in my place, and carry out your duties. This house is yours. Remain here in a good condition."

The twentieth remedy

You who are sick and seeking a remedy for your ills! Illness is of two kinds. One kind is real; the other is imaginary. As for the real kind, the All-Wise Healer of Majesty has stored up in His mighty pharmacy of the earth a remedy for every illness. Without illness, how can those remedies be known and enjoyed? The Religion requires that medicines should be used in treatment, but we should know that their effect and the cure are from God Almighty. It is He Who gives the cure, and it is He Who provides the medicine.

Following the recommendations of skilful, God-conscious doctors is an important form of treatment. For most illnesses arise from abuses, a lack of abstinence, extravagance, vice, dissipation, and indifference and a lack of care. A God-conscious doctor will certainly give advice and orders that are not contrary to Islamic precepts. They will forbid abuses and extravagance, and give consolation. The sick person has confidence in their recommendations and consolation, and the illness wanes, giving a feeling of relief in place of distress.

But when it comes to illnesses that are imaginary, the most effective medicine of all is to give it no importance. The more importance is given to it, the more it grows and swells. If no importance is given, the illness lessens and fades away. The more bees are disturbed, the more they swarm around a person's head, while if they are paid no attention, they disperse. Also, the more attention one pays to a piece of string waving in front of one's eyes in the darkness, the more it disturbs one and causes one to flee from it like a madman. While if you pay it no attention, you can see that it is an ordinary bit of string and not a snake, and you will laugh at your fear and anxiety.

If the groundless worry about one's health continues for a long time, it is transformed into reality. It is an evil ailment for the nervous and those given to groundless fears and worries; such people make a mountain out of a molehill and their morale is destroyed. In particular, if they encounter unkind and unfair "half" doctors, their worries are provoked and increase. If they are rich, they lose their wealth, or else they lose their wits, or their health.

The twenty-first remedy

You, brother or sister in faith, who are sick! You are suffering physical pain because of your illness, but a significant spiritual pleasure which will remove the effect of your physical pain surrounds you. For if you have a father, mother, or relatives, their most pleasurable compassion towards you, which you have long forgotten, will be awakened and you will see again their kind looks which you received in childhood. In addition, the friends around you who have remained veiled and hidden will look again towards you with love through the attraction of illness. In the face of these, your physical pain is infinitesimal. Also, those whom you serve proudly and from whom you try to receive appreciation now serve you kindly due to your illness, and thus you have become a master of your masters. Furthermore, since you have attracted towards yourself the fellow feeling and human tenderness of people, you have found many helpful friends and kind companions who expect nothing in return. Again, you have received from your illness the order to rest from many exhausting duties, and you are taking a rest. Certainly, in the face of these spiritual pleasures, your minor pain should lead you to thanks, not to complaint.

The twenty-second remedy

You, brother or sister in faith, who suffer a severe illness such as paralysis! Firstly, I give you the good news that for believers paralysis is regarded as blessed. I have long heard this from saintly people, but I did not know the reason. Now, one reason occurs to me as follows:

In order to obtain the approval and good pleasure of God Almighty, and to be saved from the great dangers that this world poses to the spiritual life, and to attain eternal happiness, the people of God have chosen to follow two principles:

The first is contemplation of death. Thinking of the world as transitory and realizing that they too are transient guests in the world who have many duties, they work for the eternal life in this way.

The second: In order to be saved from the dangers of the carnal, evil-commanding soul and blind passions, they have tried to kill the evil-commanding soul through austerity, religious exercises, and asceticism.

And you, my brother or sister, who have lost the health of half your body! Without choosing to do so, you have been given these two principles, which are the cause of happiness, so that your body continually warns you against the fleeting nature of the world and reminds you that humans are mortal. The world cannot drown you anymore, nor can heedlessness close your eyes. And certainly, the carnal, evil-commanding soul cannot deceive someone in the state of half a person by vile lusts and animal appetites; that person is quickly saved from the trials of the evil-commanding soul.

Thus, through belief in and submission to God and reliance on Him, a believer can benefit in a short time from a severe illness like paralysis, rather than undergoing the severe trials of the saints. Thus an illness that is so severe becomes an exceedingly modest exchange for these gains.

The twenty-third remedy

You who are ill and unhappy, alone and a stranger! While your isolation and exile together with your illness arouse sympathy in the hardest hearts and attract kindness and compassion to you, certainly they will also attract the All-Compassionate Creator's compassion towards you, which is certain to be a substitute for the sympathy and compassion of everything else. It is He Who presents Himself to us at the start of all but one of the *sura*s of the Qur'an with the Attributes of "All-Merciful and All-Compassionate." Through one gleam of His Compassion, He causes all mothers to nurture their young with wonderful tenderness, and through one manifestation of His Mercy every spring, He fills the face of the earth with bounties. Also, with all its wonders, Paradise, which is the abode of eternal happiness, constitutes a single manifestation of His Mercy. Thus, your relation to Him through belief, your recognition of Him and entreating Him through the voice of helplessness that is found in your illness, and your loneliness in exile will surely attract His mercy towards you.

Since He exists and He looks to you, everything exists for you. Those who are truly alone and in exile are those who have no relation to Him through belief and submission, or who attach no importance to that relation.

The twenty-fourth remedy

You who tend innocent, sick children or the elderly who are like innocent children! Before you is an important commodity for the Hereafter. Carry out these tasks with zeal and endeavor! In the illnesses of innocent children there are many instances of wisdom pertaining to their worldly life. For instance, their illnesses are like exercises and drills for their delicate bodies, and the inoculations and training of the Lord, so that they may be able to withstand the tumults and upheavals of the world in the future. As is accepted by verifying scholars, like expiations for sins in adults, the illnesses of innocent children are also inoculations which will serve their spiritual life, their spiritual purification and development in the future or in the Hereafter. In addition, the merits ensuing from such illnesses are recorded in the notebook of the good deeds of the parents, and particularly of the mother who, out of compassion, prefers the health of her child to her own.

As for looking after the elderly, it is accurately reported from our Prophet, upon him be peace and blessings, and has been established by many historical events, that in addition to bringing mighty rewards, receiving the prayers of the elderly, and especially that of parents, and making their hearts happy and serving them faithfully is the means to happiness both in this world and in the Hereafter.[11] And there are many experiences that establish that a child who perfectly obeys his elderly parents will receive the same treatment from his or her children, and that a child who wounds his or her parents will not only be punished in the Hereafter, but will also be subject to many disasters in this world. Not only looking after relatives who are elderly or innocent children, but also serving will-

---

[11] al-Bukhari, "Adab" 1–6,; Muslim, "Birr" 1–6, 9, 10; at-Tirmidhi, "Da'awat" 110. (Tr.)

ingly any believing sick person, especially if that one is in need of us—since there is true brotherhood coming from belief—is a requirement of being a Muslim.

The twenty-fifth remedy

You, brother and sister Muslims, who are ill! If you desire a most beneficial, truly pleasurable, and sacred medicine, which is the cure for every illness, develop your belief! That is, through repentance and seeking God's forgiveness for your sins, and the five daily Prayers, and other duties of worship, apply to your illnesses belief—that sacred cure—and the medicine it provides.

Indeed, due to the love of this world and attachment to it, it is as if the worldly people have a sick worldly existence as big as the world. We have convincingly explained in many parts of the *Risale-i Nur* that belief immediately heals that sick existence, which, like the world itself, is subject to the blows of death and separation and "riddled" with wounds and bruises. I cut short the discussion here not to weary you.

As for the medicine of belief, it shows its effect when you carry out your religious obligations as far as is possible. Heedlessness, dissipation, carnal desires, and religiously forbidden amusements prevent the effectiveness of that remedy. Since illness removes heedlessness, reduces the appetites, and prevents one from partaking in religiously unlawful pleasures, take advantage of it. Apply the sacred medicines and lights of true belief through repentance, seeking God's forgiveness, and prayers, and supplications.

May Almighty God restore you to health and make your illnesses expiation for your sins. Amen. Amen. Amen.

> They say: "All praise and gratitude are for God, Who has guided us to this. If God had not guided us, we would certainly not have found the right way. The Messengers of our Lord did indeed come with the truth." (7: 43)

> All-Glorified are You. We have no knowledge save what You have taught us. Surely You are the All-Knowing, the All-Wise.

> O God! Bestow blessings on our master Muhammad, the medicine for hearts and their cure, the good health of bodies and their healing, the light of eyes and their light, and on his Family and Companions, and bestow on them peace.

Index